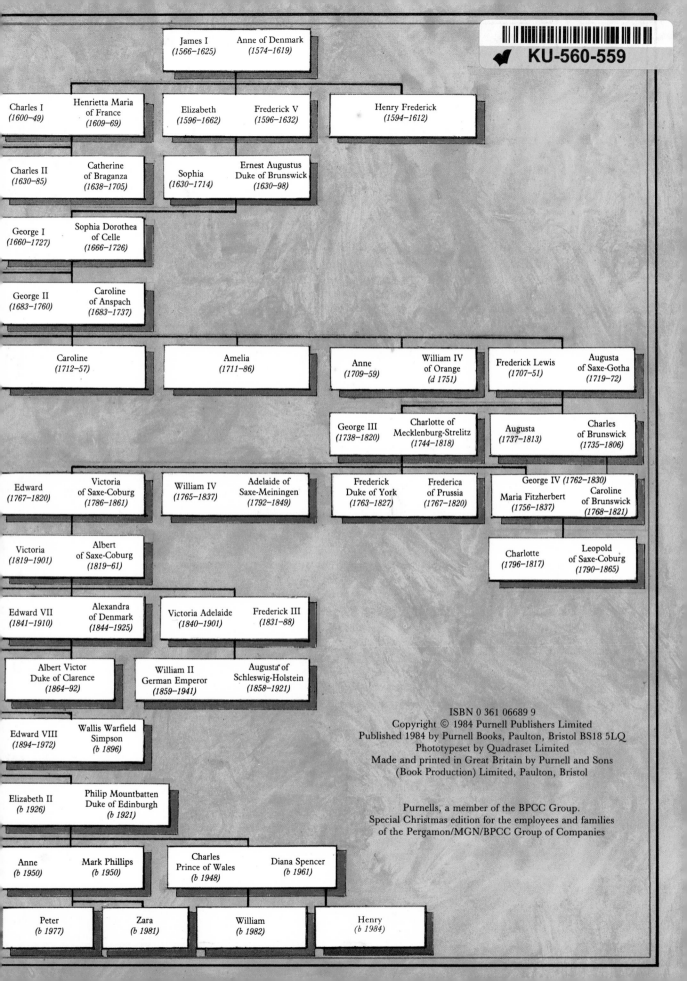

James I (1566–1625) — Anne of Denmark (1574–1619)

Charles I (1600–49) — Henrietta Maria of France (1609–69)
Elizabeth (1596–1662) — Frederick V (1596–1632)
Henry Frederick (1594–1612)

Charles II (1630–85) — Catherine of Braganza (1638–1705)
Sophia (1630–1714) — Ernest Augustus Duke of Brunswick (1630–98)

George I (1660–1727) — Sophia Dorothea of Celle (1666–1726)

George II (1683–1760) — Caroline of Anspach (1683–1737)

Caroline (1712–57)
Amelia (1711–86)
Anne (1709–59) — William IV of Orange (d 1751)
Frederick Lewis (1707–51) — Augusta of Saxe-Gotha (1719–72)

George III (1738–1820) — Charlotte of Mecklenburg-Strelitz (1744–1818)
Augusta (1737–1813) — Charles of Brunswick (1735–1806)

Edward (1767–1820) — Victoria of Saxe-Coburg (1786–1861)
William IV (1765–1837) — Adelaide of Saxe-Meiningen (1792–1849)
Frederick Duke of York (1763–1827) — Frederica of Prussia (1767–1820)
George IV (1762–1830) — Maria Fitzherbert (1756–1837) — Caroline of Brunswick (1768–1821)

Victoria (1819–1901) — Albert of Saxe-Coburg (1819–61)
Charlotte (1796–1817) — Leopold of Saxe-Coburg (1790–1865)

Edward VII (1841–1910) — Alexandra of Denmark (1844–1925)
Victoria Adelaide (1840–1901) — Frederick III (1831–88)

Albert Victor Duke of Clarence (1864–92)
William II German Emperor (1859–1941) — Augusta of Schleswig-Holstein (1858–1921)

Edward VIII (1894–1972) — Wallis Warfield Simpson (b 1896)

Elizabeth II (b 1926) — Philip Mountbatten Duke of Edinburgh (b 1921)

Anne (b 1950) — Mark Phillips (b 1950)
Charles Prince of Wales (b 1948) — Diana Spencer (b 1961)

Peter (b 1977)
Zara (b 1981)
William (b 1982)
Henry (b 1984)

ISBN 0 361 06689 9
Copyright © 1984 Purnell Publishers Limited
Published 1984 by Purnell Books, Paulton, Bristol BS18 5LQ
Phototypeset by Quadraset Limited
Made and printed in Great Britain by Purnell and Sons
(Book Production) Limited, Paulton, Bristol

Purnells, a member of the BPCC Group.
Special Christmas edition for the employees and families
of the Pergamon/MGN/BPCC Group of Companies

FROM ROBERT MAXWELL

To All Staff, Families and Friends
of the Pergamon/MGN/BPCC Group of Companies

THE ROYAL CHILDREN is the fourth volume in the series of Royal books which I have had the pleasure to send as a personal gift each Christmas to all of the people who give or have given their services to firms who are members of the Pergamon Group of Companies which, in addition to the BPCC Group and Hollis ESA Group, now also includes the illustrious Mirror Group Newspapers Ltd, with their Scottish subsidiaries the Daily Record and Sunday Mail.

As the Pergamon Group has expanded, so has the number of copies distributed of our special Christmas edition:

Volume 1	1981	The Royal Wedding	13,000 copies
Volume 2	1982	Diana Princess of Wales	14,500 copies
Volume 3	1983	Queen Elizabeth & Diana Princess of Wales	14,500 copies
Volume 4	1984	The Royal Children	25,000 copies

- so you can see what a large family we have now become! If one adds the children and other dependants of people working in our group of companies, the numbers must be in excess of 75,000.

In my message last year I predicted that "1984 will be an exciting year for us all, a year of opportunity, a year of further growth and greater success". This in fact is how it turned out, thanks to all the hard work, effort and planning by the directors, managers and workforce alike.

What about 1985? It will see us expand our business further, especially in the field of information technology and communication, cable and publishing. I am very optimistic about the immediate as well as the long-term prospects of our Group. Our services are being used by millions upon millions of people at home and abroad and we can all look forward to a bright and secure future.

A very merry Christmas and happy 1985 to you, all your family and friends.

Oxford
Christmas 1984

Robert Maxwell, Chairman
Pergamon/MGN/BPCC Group of Companies

The Royal
CHILDREN

Brenda Ralph Lewis

Purnell

Elizabeth), was Queen Mary's favourite grandchild. Like the Queen Mother, Queen Mary lived long enough to become a great-grandmother, and she appears below with Prince Charles at his christening in 1948. Unlike Charles' own son, who had to be pacified at his christening in 1982, Charles slept through the whole thing!

The Royal Family attend Sunday church on the Sandringham estate in 1972. The picture (left) shows the Queen Mother with four of her six grandchildren, the Queen's sons and daughter, Charles (left) with the Queen Mother on his arm, Andrew (centre) joking with Princess Anne and, his mother holding him firmly by the hand, Prince Edward. Prince Charles' gallantry was no mere gesture: he has a great affection for his grandmother and was delighted when his fiancée, Lady Diana Spencer, spent the weeks before their wedding at the Queen Mother's residence, Clarence House.

Although Queen Mary, paternal grandmother of the Queen, was not a demonstrative woman, there was no doubt that she was delighted with her grandchildren. She is shown here (left) with the infant Princess Elizabeth in 1926. Elizabeth, first daughter of the Duke and Duchess of York (later King George VI and Queen

he Royal Family has always been a close, affectionate family. New arrivals are no longer greeted, as infant royals once were, as perpetuators of the dynasty or, through marriage, fodder for foreign alliances. Rather, they are simply children to be cherished.

In this atmosphere, it is perfectly natural for deep regard to develop between them. Prince Charles' well-known admiration for his grandmother, the Queen Mother, is one example. Another was the closeness between the present Queen and her own grandmother, Queen Mary. The Queen, now a grandmother herself, four times over, is following in the same tradition, and there is already a host of charming pictures showing her with the children of Prince Charles and Princess Anne.

If the ever-increasing popularity of the royals, and the fact that they have escaped all the disasters to overtake so many of their European counterparts, had to be boiled down to a single source, it is this ability to give an admirable example of strong family life. It is all the more admirable because the royals have to operate under difficulties unknown to the rest of us. The chief problem for Royal Family life today is over-exposure and an intense, often intrusive, Press interest into even the most mundane of their activities. Princess Anne, Prince Edward and the Duke of Edinburgh, as well as the Princess of Wales, have all had their brushes with the Press, and the first three have become well known for their acerbic utterances on this score. Little wonder, then, that young royals are kept out of the searchlight glare of publicity as much as possible, or that the Prince and Princess of Wales have adopted the sensible strategy of arranging special Press photo-calls for their elder child, Prince William. These are sufficient to enable him to become accustomed to the cameras which will follow him about for the rest of his life, yet are limited enough not to disturb or distort his early years.

That Prince William and the other Wales children will have

In a photograph taken two years earlier, in 1970 (above), the Queen Mother steadies Lady Sarah Armstrong Jones, Princess Margaret's daughter, as she navigates her way round one of the royal corgis. Beside Sarah walks her brother, Viscount Linley. Ahead lies another family Christmas at Sandringham and, for the older royals, time off from the pressures of public life.
A new royal baby and a new grandmother. The Queen lends a helping hand with Peter Phillips as he sits on Princess Anne's lap at his christening in 1978. Peter is the Queen's first grandchild (right).
The familiar happy scene took place again in 1982 when Prince William was christened at Buckingham Palace. The picture (left) shows four royal generations. The Queen (right), by this time a grandmother for the third time, Prince Charles the proud father on the left and seated between them the equally proud great-grandmother, with the baby prince on her lap. The day was a double pleasure for the Queen Mother, for it was also her 82nd birthday, 4th August.

lives circumscribed by their royal status is obvious. Even royals further from the throne have to accept such curbs. Viscount Linley is an up-and-coming photographer and his sister, Lady Sarah Armstrong-Jones, a promising art student. However, being the children of Princess Margaret and therefore greatly favoured by birth, their chances of proving themselves in their own right are that much more difficult. Likewise, Prince Andrew may be a born sailor and a Falklands War veteran to boot, but he must still perform the same social and official duties as the rest of the 'family firm' and maybe one day accept, as his father did, that his own career might have to give way to his royal obligations.

In addition, the most ordinary events become extra-ordinary, even controversial, where the Royal Family is concerned. For instance, in 1945, the last year of the Second World War, the Queen, then Princess Elizabeth, caused quite a

The Queen Mother enjoyed a marvellously warm and close family life as a child, which goes a long way towards explaining her lifelong serenity and her knack of creating loving family relationships. The ninth of the ten children of the Earl and Countess of Strathmore, the Queen Mother, then Lady Elizabeth Bowes-Lyon, was born on 4th August 1900, and was an especially pretty and charming child. She learned early on how to be the great, yet gracious, lady and was once discovered by her mother, at age four, entertaining guests to tea as if she were the lady of the manor! This picture (above) shows the nine-year-old Lady Elizabeth in a very regal pose, dressed in 16th stir by joining the Auxiliary Territorial Service (ATS) to become No. 230873 Junior Subaltern, a driver and mechanic. The motive — encouraging girls of Elizabeth's own age to 'do their bit' for the war effort — was not doubted for a moment, but all the same, it was unusual for the Heiress Presumptive to get her hands dirty at manual labour. Some years later, when Prince Charles and Princess Anne went to school, it was almost epoch-making in a family where children, the Queen and Princess Margaret included, were educated privately at home as a matter of course. Later, Princess Anne broke new ground when she qualified for the Olympics equestrian team, even though a precedent of sorts had been set by her grandfather King George VI, who once played in a doubles match at Wimbledon. And in 1981, when Anne chose to call her daughter, the Queen's first grand-daughter, Zara, there was much comment about the break this represented in a family which has a limited, traditional choice of names.

Similarly, Prince Edward's grades at school and Charles' university degree have become newspaper headlines when in an ordinary family the information would be of interest only to relatives, friends and prospective employers.

It is also significant that in spite of all the royals' informality and their expertise at the 'common touch' which so delights their subjects, the restraints on them become very visible when it comes to their marriages. The Royal Family have suffered two serious upheavals on this score. First in 1936 when King Edward VIII abdicated rather than give up the 'unacceptable' wife he wished to marry, secondly in 1955, at the time of

century costume at Glamis Castle. Dressing up and play-acting has always been a royal activity, and both Princess Elizabeth (now the Queen) and Princess Margaret used to perform regularly for their parents in plays of their own devising.

The main photograph shows Lady Elizabeth two years earlier, in 1907, looking charmingly romantic with her smocked dress and spray of blossom. She is in a slightly more pensive mood in the attractive miniature in the top right-hand corner, which dates from 1906. Right up until her engagement, Lady Elizabeth wore her hair long with a fringe, as shown in this very tranquil portrait (right).

In her adolescence she helped nurse the wounded who came to Glamis Castle during the First World War, which broke out on her 14th birthday in August 1914.

The picture on the left was taken on May 1st, 1923, in the gardens of Polesden Lacey, near Dorking, Surrey. It was here that the twenty-three-year-old Elizabeth spent her honeymoon, with her husband the Duke of York, later to become George VI. As a mature young woman, she displays again the poise and serenity which characterise all the portraits on these pages.

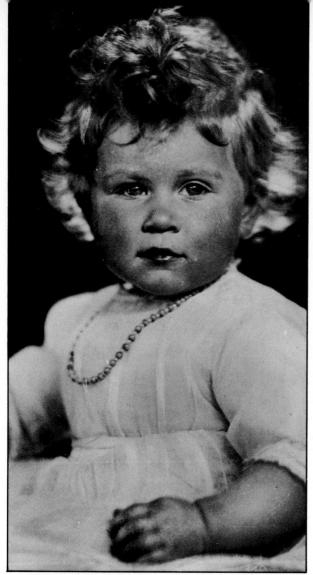

Princess Margaret's doomed attachment to the divorced Peter Townsend. These experiences have sunk deep into royal consciousness and this was why the Princess of Wales had to have a blameless personal background before she could marry Prince Charles. Not too long ago, in fact, her parents' divorce would have put her, quite literally, out of court. However, there could be no concessions on her own past. There could be no risk that some former boyfriend might come out of the woodwork to embarrass the Royal Family. In fact, Charles was once forced to give up a young lady of whom he was particularly fond when her cupboard was found to contain a skeleton.

It is, however, greatly to the Royal Family's credit that

Fifty years ago, these two delightful Princesses, Elizabeth seen (above) at the age of one in 1927, and Margaret, seen here (far right, bottom) at two, in 1932, were the darlings of the nation. King George V, their grandfather, was on the throne then and though the princesses were third and fourth in the line of succession, there was no hint that the elder would one day be Queen. The Press, the public, their parents and grandparents all adored the 'little Princesses', and pictures of them in the newspapers or cinema newsreels were as popular then as photographs of Princess Diana or Prince William are now. Princess Elizabeth and Princess Margaret Rose (she later insisted on dropping the second name) lived a happy, secure life and their pictures show that royals, too, could have fun. Princess Elizabeth is shown

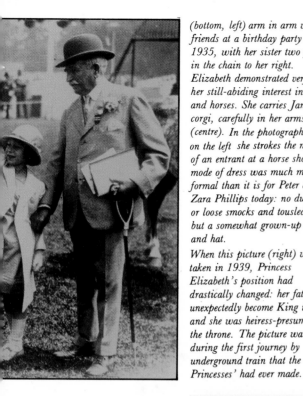

(bottom, left) arm in arm with friends at a birthday party in 1935, with her sister two places in the chain to her right. Elizabeth demonstrated very early her still-abiding interest in dogs and horses. She carries Jane, the corgi, carefully in her arms (centre). In the photograph on the left she strokes the muzzle of an entrant at a horse show. Her mode of dress was much more formal than it is for Peter and Zara Phillips today: no dungarees or loose smocks and tousled hair, but a somewhat grown-up coat and hat.

When this picture (right) was taken in 1939, Princess Elizabeth's position had drastically changed: her father had unexpectedly become King in 1936 and she was heiress-presumptive to the throne. The picture was taken during the first journey by underground train that the 'little Princesses' had ever made.

despite the personal frustrations their status can cause, the royal children are reared to be such likeable, well-balanced people, dutiful in an unstuffy way, genuinely interested in those around them and showing the world a near-impeccable public face nicely stamped with their own personalities. Of course the royal image slips a bit from time to time, for the perennial requirement to be gracious is hard to maintain. However, this simply proves they're human and they are held in such regard that no one really minds. If Peter Phillips is pictured giving his sister a clip on the ear, it's looked on as naughty but normal, to give only one example.

Admittedly, normality is not that easy to come by for the royals. Prince Philip once named bringing up his children to be

Because of the ten-year gap between Princess Anne and Prince Andrew, the Queen and the Duke of Edinburgh have, in a sense, produced two families and the family photo album covers more years than is usually the case. In fact, nearly thirteen years separate these pictures of Prince Charles and Prince Andrew as babies. Charles, solemnly concerned with a fluffy rabbit, is shown at 16 months in April 1950 (left). Andrew (above), showing the world the smile he still retains, is pictured with the Queen in September 1962, when he was two and a half. Prince Charles, seen as a schoolboy three months before his thirteenth birthday in 1962 (right), was almost grown up by the time his second brother, Edward, was born in 1964. Naturally enough, Charles and Princess Anne were close friends, both as toddlers (above) and later on. At 15 and 14, they shared the fun of the fair at Olympia in

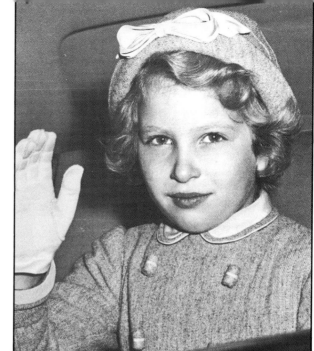

1964 (below). Charles has already chosen his bumper car. Anne has an eye on hers.

Charles, aged four, attended his mother's coronation on 2nd June 1953 and here he has a point explained to him by his grandmother, while his Aunt Margaret looks on (below, right). Charles was, by then, heir to the throne though he probably didn't realise it. Years later, he said: "I didn't suddenly sit up in my pram one day and say 'Gosh, I'm going to be King!' The realisation sort of grew on me."

Despite the fact that she is probably the most informal of the royals, Anne learned early how to give the royal wave. She is seen making a gracious job of it (right) at the age of seven as she greets the crowd at a London railway station.

reasonable human beings as his most important task as a parent. His and the Queen's success in doing just that was, in its turn, called "a bloody miracle" by Philip's uncle Lord Louis Mountbatten, and there's quite a deal of truth in that. Royal children have always tended to become the darlings of the nation — as the 'little princesses', the Queen and Princess Margaret were fifty years ago, and they could easily become thoroughly spoiled and imperious.

The present outgoing image of the Royal Family and the affection that exists between the generations is very much the creation of the Queen Mother. Like her own mother, the Countess of Strathmore, she has a talent for family life which first of all provided a loving haven for her husband, the late King George VI. King George, who was Albert, Duke of York when he married Lady Elizabeth Bowes-Lyon in 1923, had come from an overly strict, even harsh background. His father, George V, is reputed to have declared: "I was afraid of my father and I'm going to make darned sure my children are afraid of me!" Though George V was not really the martinet this suggests — he and his wife, Queen Mary, were simply unable to express their love for their children or, indeed, each other — the Duke of York's childhood proved so arduous for the shy, physically frail and sensitive youngster that he suffered

Princess Anne has always been an outdoor girl. Here she is on her sixth birthday (below), 15th August 1956, stepping ashore to enjoy a picnic on South Uist, one of the Outer Hebridean islands of Scotland.

from ulcers and a stammer. Happily, his marriage proved the making of him. The loving, relaxed environment which his wife created for him and their two daughters was a revelation to the Duke and both the girls grew up with the great advantage of having parents who adored them and each other.

The feelings were mutual. Princess Elizabeth, or 'Lilibet' as she was known, was extremely close to her father and without strain or tension learned from him the arts of the monarchy she was destined to inherit in 1952. Numerous delightful pictures of father and daughter together testify as to how genuine their affection was for each other. From her mother, Elizabeth inherited her love of animals and the country life as well as a quiet, steady sense of duty and an understanding of the special responsibilities conferred by royal blood. Above all, Princess Elizabeth saw in her parents' relationship how a loving marriage worked. She drew her own conclusions from the lesson, and years later, Prince Charles was able to say that he aimed to be as happy in marriage as his parents were.

This was in itself no mean feat when the Duke of Edinburgh, a strong and dominant character, has had to take a back seat to

Prince Andrew, a typical five-year-old, tries hill-climbing at Frogmore (right).

his wife's position and is placed in the official order of precedence after his own son.

Sadly, though, Prince Charles is the only one of the Queen's children who was able to get to know his grandfather, King George VI, to any extent. The king died, aged 56, on 6th February 1952, less than three months after Charles' third birthday, the previous 14th November. Princess Anne, born 15th August 1950, was not yet eighteen months old.

The Queen's accession to the throne at the age of 25 curtailed her plans for a large family, and eight years passed before Prince Andrew arrived on 19th February 1960. Charles was eleven and Anne nine, and soon after Andrew's birth the Queen told her husband that they would have to provide a playmate for him, closer in age. The playmate was Prince Edward, born on 10th March 1964.

For the Queen Mother, Edward was a fifth grandchild. Princess Margaret, who married in May 1960, had given birth to Viscount Linley on 3rd November 1961, and was expecting her second child a few weeks after the Queen. Early 1964, in

The Queen leaves for Balmoral where the Royal Family spend their summer holidays and where they are, by recognised agreement with the Press, left alone to enjoy themselves. The picture below was taken in August 1964 and shows the Queen with her 'second family', Prince Andrew, then aged four, and baby Prince Edward. That summer was the first get-together of all her grandchildren for the Queen Mother. Prince Charles, Princess Anne and Princess Margaret's children, Viscount Linley and baby Sarah Armstrong-Jones, then three months old, were also at Balmoral.

fact, saw no less than four new royals arrive — Princess Alexandra's son James, the Duchess of Kent's daughter Helen, Prince Edward, and the last, Princess Margaret's daughter Sarah. The Queen Mother's brood of six grandchildren was now complete, but she could of course look forward to her next role, as great-grandmother. Princess Anne, the first royal grandchild to marry, in 1973, had decided ideas of her own about not starting a family too soon. ''I think couples should get to know each other properly before they start having children,'' she said.

If Anne went against the normal royal trend by having her first child after four years of marriage, instead of one or two, she followed another tradition: like the Queen, Princess Margaret, Princess Alexandra, the Duchess of Kent, the Duchess of Gloucester and Princess Michael, it was boy first for Anne and girl next. Anne's son, Master Peter Phillips — he has no title because his father is a commoner — arrived on 15th November 1977, the day after his parents' fourth wedding anniversary. The arrival of Zara, Princess Anne's daughter on 15th May 1981 was somewhat overshadowed by the imminent marriage, set for 29th July, of Prince Charles and Lady Diana Spencer. Poor Zara was, in fact, christened almost unnoticed the day before the wedding.

When Charles and Diana married, one thing was quite certain. Diana had already put ''children of course'' at the top of her list of priorities when asked about her future plans on her engagement. Diana's love of children and her talent for

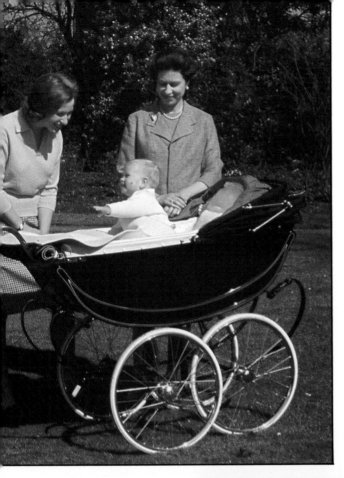

The following year, in April 1965, Prince Edward, at 13 months, was sitting up and taking notice at Frogmore (below left) where the Royal Family were enjoying a spring holiday (left). This very self-contained young man, studying form, is Prince Edward at the age of eight. He was photographed (centre, below) at the cross-country section of the Badminton Horse Trials in April 1972.

The Braemar Games, in early September, normally see the only public appearance of the Royal Family during their summer holiday at Balmoral. (Below) In 1966, Prince Andrew, Princess Anne and Prince Charles were pictured with their grandmother at the Games, where the royals occupy a special green box-enclosure.

handling them had been evident from her work as a kindergarten teacher, and it was this homeloving quality which particularly endeared her to the Queen and made her so suitable a wife for the heir to the throne. Prince William was born on 21st June 1982, eleven months after his parents' wedding and with him there began what is, in effect, a new Royal Family.

''Give us another one!'' someone saucily yelled to Charles from the crowd of well-wishers teeming around St. Mary's Hospital, Paddington, on the night William was born. Two and a half years later 'another one' duly arrived and the Queen was presented with another grandchild. Two children is unlikely to be the limit of the Wales family. Diana is, after all, still only 23 and always intended to have 'lots and lots' of children. In addition Prince Andrew and after him Prince Edward as well as Princess Margaret's children are now in line for next to the altar. All in all, this makes the description 'Royal Grandchildren' only the story so far, with many more episodes to follow.

For a royal prince to take a wife
from the ranks of the English
aristocracy is, historically, nothing
unusual. Princess Diana is
therefore the latest in a long line
and has a lustre of her own in her
descent from the Duke of
Marlborough, Winston
Churchill's famous ancestor.
Diana was a charming, pretty
child, as can be seen from this
picture of her (far right) in 1972
with her guinea-pig Peanuts. The
photograph was taken at the
Sandringham Show.
Most pictures of Diana's
childhood were taken by her
adoring father, Earl Spencer.
Here he is watching Diana and
her brother Charles enjoying
a camel ride at the zoo
(right). The Princess

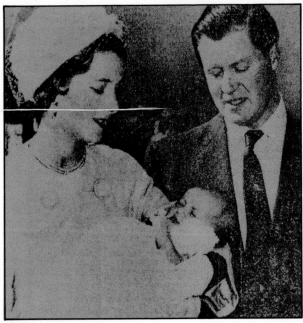

of Wales is the third child of Earl
Spencer and his first wife, the
former Frances Roche. The
photograph (above) showing the
baby Diana with her parents at
her christening did, however, hide
a great sadness in the family. The
Spencers had lost a child only the
previous year and their relationship
never really recovered from the
blow. The Princess, sadly, grew
up in a broken home which had
been torn apart by a particularly
controversial divorce.
Despite this drawback, though,
Diana grew up to be a pretty,
fair-haired, marvellously blue-eyed
girl with a warm nature. She was
something of the girl-next-door for

the Royal Family, for she spent
much of her childhood at Park
House on the Sandringham Estate
and her childhood chums were
Prince Andrew and Prince
Edward, both of whom were, like
her, born in the early 1960s.
Prince Charles took on the rôle of
admired elder brother, and he
remembers Diana from those days
as a "rather splendid" 16-year-
old. The photograph (right) shows
Diana dressed as a bridesmaid
for her sister Jane's wedding in
April 1978.
At school, Diana's forte was not
academic, but lay more in her
interest and empathy with people,
particularly children.

Late in 1980, when her name was first seriously linked with that of Prince Charles, the most popular pictures of her showed Diana as the working girl, at the Young England Kindergarten in London's Pimlico (right). The delightful main picture shows her with two of the children in the garden of the school. She has been back to visit them several times since she became Princess of Wales. In addition to working at the school, Diana spent one day a week looking after the child of a close friend.

After her engagement to Prince Charles, the Press were quick to photograph Diana with the small children she so loves, like this little boy she took care of at a polo match (far left).

Princess Anne, her husband Captain Mark Phillips and their children, Peter and Zara, lead a decidedly country-based life at their home in Gloucestershire. Their house, Gatcombe Park, is the sort of place where you find wellies in the hall! The Phillips family is very much a farming family that has royal connections rather than the other way around, and of course horses play an important part in their lives. Peter Phillips, now aged six, is often pictured at horse shows. Here he is pulling his father's coat tails at Badminton (right) and watching Princess Anne on horseback as she clears a hurdle (below).

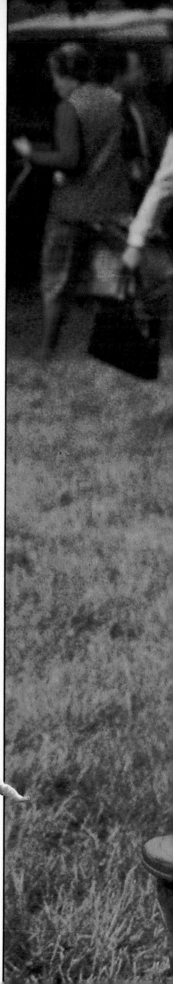

Zara, too, has been introduced to the country life very early. Quite fearlessly, she holds the rein of a horse which towers above her at Tetbury in September 1983 (far left, bottom) when she was less than two and a half years old.

The Phillips family album contains many delightful and informal pictures. Here is Zara (bottom, left) dancing along beside her mother in a photograph taken at the Windsor Horse Trials. Peter, a very handsome child with beautiful fair hair, sits watching the proceedings at Windsor Park (main picture) and, kitted out for the saddle, looks determined to enjoy himself at Sandringham (below).

Peter is seen on horseback (main picture) accompanied by his father and one of the many family dogs, again at Sandringham. Peter's personal pony is called Trigger. Both Peter and Zara are rumbustious children and it is not unknown for Peter to have his bottom smacked in public by Princess Anne and be taken home in disgrace. A certain amount of rough and tumble is, of course, permitted. This picture (top, left) shows Peter's method of making friends! At home, Peter's favourite trick is to get himself as dirty as possible in the farmyard and then do a dance, still clad in his wellies, on the beautifully polished rosewood grand piano. It's not all mud and wellies, of course: here (top, right) is Peter more formally clad when attending a wedding. Zara, who turned three in May 1984, is too young as yet for real high-jinks, but she has made a start, as can be seen in this picture of her with her brother and nanny (above). There are also quieter moments, displaying the charm of a child's country life, as this picture of Zara standing in the grass shows (left).

An alert photographer took this series of pictures showing Peter Phillips launching himself with gusto into a cartwheel, but not quite succeeding! The setting for all this activity was Badminton in 1982.

The camera was on hand again when Zara made friends with one of the horses at the Badminton Horse Trials in 1984 (far right, top). A moment after this picture was taken, Zara dived between the horse's forelegs to have a closer look at its hooves! But her interest in animals is not confined to horses, as the main picture shows.

Formal pictures of either Peter or Zara are still rare, although Peter did not have much say in this reminder of his royal descent, which was taken at his christening in Buckingham Palace in 1978 (right).

Queen's grandchildren or no, the Phillipses are determined to give their son and daughter as carefree a childhood as possible, untouched by royal trappings. At the age of three, just like other children, both Peter and Zara attended nursery schools and both are finding their friends among the Gloucestershire farming gentry whose farms are close to the Phillips's 700 acres at Gatcombe Park.

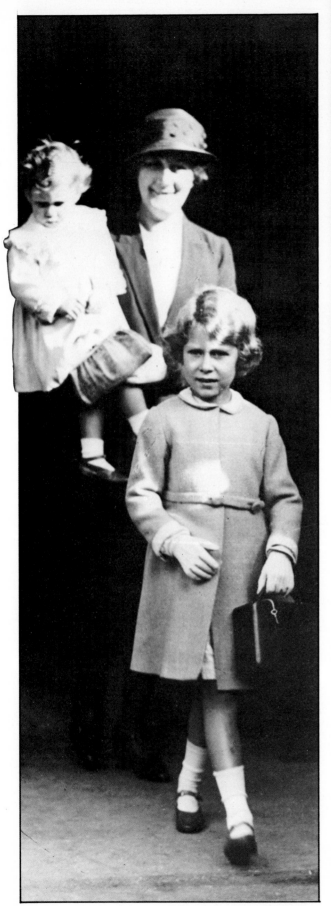

Spending so much of their time in the glare of publicity means that the Royal Family place special value on their holidays. At Sandringham, where they spend Christmas, or Balmoral, where they usually go in summer, or at Royal Lodge Windsor or Frogmore, the royals can get together simply as people and enjoy the company of their children. Like any other family, they can relax and enjoy themselves. Balmoral has always been a special royal favourite. Queen Victoria thought it the most beautiful place on earth and the Royal Family still gathers there regularly. Here (left) Princess Elizabeth, the future Queen, and Princess Margaret arrive at Ballater Station, bound for Balmoral in 1932. Margaret celebrated her second birthday, 21st August, during their stay. A generation later (above), Prince Charles and Princess Anne make the traditional short break from the holiday at Balmoral to attend the Braemar Games, in 1960. (Right) At Royal Lodge,

Windsor, in 1942, Princess Margaret and her sister set out on their bicycles in search of some rural peace and quiet. These were the years of the Second World War, when breaks in the countryside were particularly important as a rest from the strain of living in London.

Nearly thirty years later, in 1968, the Queen, the Duke of Edinburgh and their four children pose in the grounds at Windsor (right). The newest arrival, Prince Edward, then aged four, sits between his parents, with Prince Andrew at the Queen's left and Charles and Anne standing behind.

A few months later, Edward was pictured hand in hand with his mother when the Royal Family attended Christmas Day service at St. George's Chapel, Windsor (below right).

Holidays over (below, far right): Prince Andrew and his cousin, Lord Linley, arrive from Sandringham at Liverpool Street Station, London in 1971.

When the Prince and Princess of Wales undertook their first major tour abroad in 1983, there was no question of leaving their baby son behind. Prince William therefore experienced his first royal tour before he was even a year old, a record even in the extensively-travelled Royal Family. Nanny Barbara Barnes went too, of course, and cared for William at Woomergama while his parents did their official rounds. Here's William arriving with Nanny Barnes at Alice Springs (above) where he was soon handed over to his parents for photographs to be taken (above, right).
Prince William soon acquired the knack of the royal wave which delighted the crowds when the Prince and Princess took him driving through the streets during their tour. There was a photo call

for William at Government House in Auckland, New Zealand, where he went crawlabout for the Press (below, left) and even managed a jig.

At the time of the royal tour, there was some talk in Australia about replacing the monarchy (the Queen is Queen of Australia) with a republic. However, the Aussies' excited reception for Charles, Diana and William probably put that idea back by many years. Although his first birthday was still some time away, Prince William had already had time to get used to that perennial royal companion, the camera. These pictures (right and below) were taken at Christmas 1982, when he was six months old, and this photograph (below, right) shows the baby prince arriving by air for the royal summer holiday in Scotland in August 1983.

Prince William had his very own appointment with the Press a few months later, in December, when he spent several minutes out in the crisp winter air together with his parents (above and below).

William showed a wary curiosity when his father explained the workings of the camera to him, and at one stage made a bolt for the garden gate and had to be brought back by Prince Charles.

Another photo-call in the garden, at Kensington Palace, took place to mark William's second birthday, 21st June 1984 (left). Prince Charles gives a hand to get his young son swinging (below) but a persuasive word from mum is needed (below, centre) to get William to face the lenses. Princess Diana also had to intervene at William's christening on 4th August 1982, at Buckingham Palace (below, right), when she had to give him her little finger to suck in order to stop him crying.
(Right) With his cousins Zara (left) and Peter Phillips (right) flanking him, William gets used to that familiar royal stamping ground, the balcony at Buckingham Palace, as the royals greet the crowds after the Trooping of the Colour in June 1984.

Princess Margaret came later to motherhood than most of the royal ladies. She married at 29 and had her first child at 31. Even so, she certainly thrives on it as this delightful picture (right, bottom) of the Princess with her daughter, Lady Sarah Armstrong-Jones, on her lap and her son, Viscount Linley, beside her amply demonstrates. The Princess and her children were returning from Sandringham in 1968.

Royal or not, Viscount Linley and Lady Sarah know how to tuck into ice lollies. This picture was taken at the Badminton Horse Trials in April 1970 (far right, bottom).

Serious business for the Armstrong-Jones children. Princess Margaret's son and daughter are seen in their school uniforms in 1971. The two children, who resemble each other quite remarkably, were photographed by their father, Lord Snowdon, in a picture released on the day Lady Sarah, 7, started school in London (right, top).

Royal cousins. Lady Sarah is seen here with her cousin, Prince Edward, at Windsor Great Park. They were born in the same year, 1964, only seven weeks apart. This picture was taken in 1971 (far right, top).

Not surprisingly, both the children of Princess Margaret and Lord Snowdon seem to have inherited their parents' artistic talents. Lady Sarah is seen here (far right) starting her first term at the Camberwell School of Art in September 1982. Her brother, who prefers to be known simply as David Linley, has entered the furniture business and has also followed his brilliant father into the world of photography. In 1983 the magazine Vogue published a set of his pictures.

One of the greatest points of public interest when there's a new royal arrival is the choice of nanny for the new baby. Until the Princess of Wales chose the young, attractive Barbara Barnes as nanny for Prince William, most royal nannies followed a familiar formula: usually middle aged, uniformed and looking not at all put out by the occasional prospect of correcting the royal behaviour. In a word, the royal nanny was at one time quite a formidable prospect. Princess Elizabeth's nanny certainly looks as if she will stand no nonsense as she takes her young charge out for a ride in 1927 (top, left). The future Queen, then the only child of the Duke and Duchess of York (later King George VI and Queen Elizabeth), was about a year old. ''Crawfie'', the best known of all the royal nannies, arrived on the scene when the Queen and her sister were older and their father had become King.

Prince Charles' nanny, Sister Helen Rowe, looks loving but capable as she contemplates the baby in her charge in December 1948. The pictures were taken at Charles' christening, at Buckingham Palace (top centre and top right, facing page). (Below) The cheery, pleasant nanny seen here with Princess Anne and Prince Andrew is Miss Mabel Anderson, who became a member of the royal household in 1948, the year of Prince Charles' birth. Mabel Anderson looked after both Anne and Andrew and, in 1977, when Anne had her first child, Miss Anderson was chosen automatically to be his nanny. A charming picture, and an

informal one, of Barbara Barnes, Prince William's nanny (above). Out walking with nanny in this photograph taken at Balmoral (main picture) are Prince William and Zara Phillips. Zara is only 13 months older than William.

Fashion for the royal children has changed enormously since the 'little Princesses' were so carefully dressed for their public appearances forty and fifty years ago. When it came to portraits (far left, above), it was definitely frilly party best for the two girls.

However, this curious little figure (left, above) clad in frilly toque, wide skirts and button-up boots is not a girl, as one might imagine: it's Prince George, later King George V, in the normal attire for small boys as it was over a century ago.

The delightful photograph (left) shows Princess Anne, almost three, and Prince Charles, aged four, all dressed up for their mother's coronation in 1953. Prince Andrew and Prince Edward make a matching pair (above). They are pictured at Liverpool Street Station in 1966. Off-duty, however, the royals appear in sweatshirts and dungarees: this is Prince Edward at Windsor Great Park in 1971 (far right). It's sweater and jeans for Peter Phillips (right) and romper suit and matching striped T-shirt for William on his birthday photo-call in 1984 (right, above). It's no accident,

though, that informal royal fashions like these look as if they came out of the high street superstore: whatever William wears becomes fashion.

The crowds began to gather outside St. Mary's Hospital, Paddington, early on the morning of Saturday 15th September 1984 when it became known that the Princess of Wales had entered the hospital for the birth of her second child. It was another boy, born at 4.20 p.m., and as the news reached the outside world the waiting crowds cheered.
Left: Buckingham Palace gates display official notice of the birth and *(below left)* congratulations and cuddly toys begin to pour in. The large box presented by the local police station contained a huge Paddington Bear.
Right: Prince William was introduced to his new brother the day after the birth. Despite all the excitement, he didn't forget to give the crowds a royal wave.
Main picture and below: Only twenty-two hours after the birth,

the Princess takes her new son home. His names have now been announced — Henry Charles Albert David, to be known within the Royal Family as Harry.
Opposite and below: Little Prince Henry faces the camera at just twenty-eight days old. These photographs of the happy family were taken by Lord Snowdon at Kensington Palace in October 1984.
Right: A confident William gives his new brother a few tips on posing for the camera.

Queen Elizabeth II

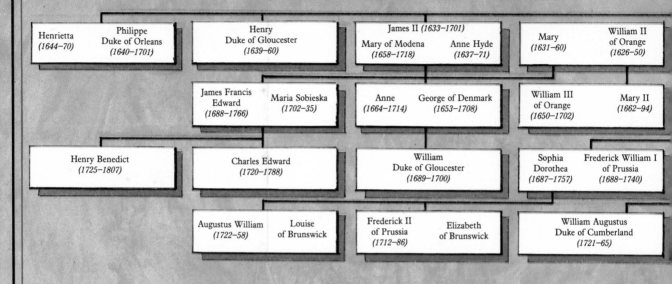

| Henrietta *(1644–70)* | Philippe Duke of Orleans *(1640–1701)* | Henry Duke of Gloucester *(1639–60)* | James II *(1633–1701)* Mary of Modena *(1658–1718)* / Anne Hyde *(1637–71)* | Mary *(1631–60)* | William II of Orange *(1626–50)* |

| James Francis Edward *(1688–1766)* / Maria Sobieska *(1702–35)* | Anne *(1664–1714)* George of Denmark *(1653–1708)* | William III of Orange *(1650–1702)* | Mary II *(1662–94)* |

| Henry Benedict *(1725–1807)* | Charles Edward *(1720–1788)* | William Duke of Gloucester *(1689–1700)* | Sophia Dorothea *(1687–1757)* / Frederick William I of Prussia *(1688–1740)* |

| Augustus William *(1722–58)* / Louise of Brunswick | Frederick II of Prussia *(1712–86)* / Elizabeth of Brunswick | William Augustus Duke of Cumberland *(1721–65)* |

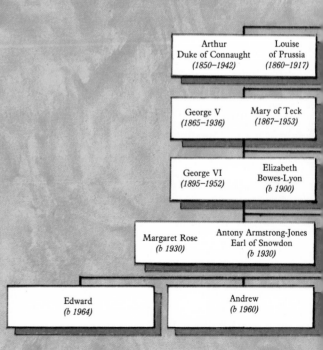

| Arthur Duke of Connaught *(1850–1942)* | Louise of Prussia *(1860–1917)* |

| George V *(1865–1936)* | Mary of Teck *(1867–1953)* |

| George VI *(1895–1952)* | Elizabeth Bowes-Lyon *(b 1900)* |

| Margaret Rose *(b 1930)* | Antony Armstrong-Jones Earl of Snowdon *(b 1930)* |

| Edward *(b 1964)* | Andrew *(b 1960)* |